T0285990

IMAGES
of America

ELLSWORTH
AIR FORCE BASE

IMAGES
of America

ELLSWORTH
AIR FORCE BASE

Joseph T. Page II

ARCADIA
PUBLISHING

Published by Arcadia Publishing
Charleston, South Carolina

Printed in the United States of America

Library of Congress Control Number: 2021934538

For all general information, please contact Arcadia Publishing:
Telephone 843-853-2070
Fax 843-853-0044
E-mail sales@arcadiapublishing.com
For customer service and orders:
Toll-Free 1-888-313-2665

Visit us on the Internet at www.arcadiapublishing.com

This book is dedicated to the men, women, and children of Ellsworth Air Force Base.

CONTENTS

ACKNOWLEDGMENTS

Thanks to the US Air Force for providing two kind, generous, and extremely competent points of contact for this book: Carla Pampe (Air Force Global Strike Command) and MSgt Corenthia Keyonna Fennell (US Air Force Book Support Office). I hope all of my future books receive the high level of support they have provided.

The 44th Missile Wing (44 MW) Facebook group Black Hills Bandits gave enthusiastic support for the project. It was great to hear the stories, gripes, and jibes from fellow Minuteman missileers and maintainers. Bruce Stovall provided two images from his missile time at Ellsworth, and Eric Leonard, superintendent for the National Park Service's Minuteman Missile National Historic Site, was instrumental in providing oral history interviews of former 44 MW missileers. Kudos to Kent Pillatsch for providing images of missile hardware at the base. A special shout-out to "Groundskeeper Pete," the force behind the Chromehooves website, detailing Ellsworth Air Force Base's Titan history. Greg Ogletree gave critical feedback on the book, for which I am extremely grateful. His corrections eliminated more than a few errors.

Stacia Bannerman at Arcadia Publishing provided me another opportunity to bring Air Force history to light. I am extremely grateful for her patience and understanding.

Thanks to the baristas at Satellite Coffee's Wyoming (Avenue) location: Sam, Jon, Billy, Daniel, and Benji.

As always, thanks to my wife, Kim, and children for being the motivational support behind my writing projects. Finally, a kind acknowledgment to the four cats who love walking on my keyboard as I type.

INTRODUCTION

Located 10 miles northeast of Rapid City, South Dakota, Ellsworth Air Force Base occupies a unique place in Air Force history. At times throughout its nearly eight decades of service, the base served as a training location for heavy bomber aircrews, the location of an atomic (and later thermonuclear) weapons operational storage site, the home to two legs of the nuclear triad (bombers and missiles), and now, a nesting location for both manned and unmanned aerial vehicles. Over the decades, Ellsworth has maintained a ready fleet of aircraft for the defense of the United States, supported by thousands of military men and women.

RAPID CITY ARMY AIR BASE

Increasing global tensions in the late 1930s brought the US military out of years of malaise that began after World War I. The strongest indication of the growing strategic importance of military air power was the expansion of the US Army Air Corps' military aviation program, which required construction of hundreds of new facilities across the nation. The number of aviation-related garrisons grew five-fold, from 21 to 114, between 1937 and 1941, increasing even more after the attack on Pearl Harbor, Hawaii, on December 7, 1941.

Rapid City was one of the locations inspected by the Army for future aviation facilities. After extensive lobbying by local civic leaders and South Dakota's congressional delegation, the Army selected a low plateau east of Rapid City as the future air base location in December 1941. The War Department established Rapid City Army Air Base (RCAAB) on January 2, 1942, and construction started immediately. The base saw rapid construction of several dozen wood-framed buildings along with three concrete runways for the training of B-17 Flying Fortress crews. Aircrew training continued until the end of World War II.

The signing of the National Security Act on September 18, 1947, established the United States Air Force (USAF) as a separate military branch within the Department of Defense. While the service's name change was immediate, Rapid City's military airfield went through many names that did not last long. From mid-1947 to mid-1948, the base went through four name changes:

Rapid City Army Air Field (September 1946 to November 28, 1947)
Rapid City Air Field (November 28, 1947, to January 13, 1948)
Weaver Air Force Base (January 13, 1948, to June 24, 1948)
Rapid City Air Force Base (June 24, 1948, to June 1, 1953)

In 1947, the base became the home of the 28th Bombardment Wing (28 BMW) flying B-29 Superfortress bombers and was declared a permanent installation a year later. This status change enabled additional funding for facility and runway upgrades. In 1949, facility and runway improvements were completed for the 28 BMW conversion from the B-29 to the B-36 Peacemaker.

The base's final name change came nearly five years later in response to a tragic aircraft accident. On March 18, 1953, a 28th Strategic Reconnaissance Wing (28 SRW) RB-36 crashed in Newfoundland, Canada, killing all crewmembers aboard. Among the plane's fatalities was the commander of the 28 SRW, Brig. Gen. Richard E. Ellsworth. In June, Pres. Dwight D. Eisenhower presided over the ceremony renaming RCAFB to Ellsworth Air Force Base.

RUSHMORE AIR FORCE STATION (1952–1962)

The large buildup of atomic weapons during the early Cold War provided logistical challenges to weapon designers charged with providing the bombs to Strategic Air Command's (SAC's) aircraft bombardment fleet. In 1946, the Atomic Energy Act created the Atomic Energy Commission (AEC) to maintain custody of all atomic weapons and storage infrastructure to support the stockpile. The civilian agency was created to alleviate any fears of the military having a monopoly on atomic (and later thermonuclear) weaponry. Early atomic weapons had nuclear and non-nuclear components stored separately and only joined together just before their intended use—before being loaded onto an aircraft or while flying toward the target. Military personnel would perform this arming function during nuclear combat but would otherwise not have custody of the weapons beforehand. AEC civilian employees would provide stockpile management and train the military in maintenance and weapon assembly.

In the late 1940s, the AEC and Armed Forces Special Weapons Project (AFSWP) agreed to a consolidation of nuclear weapon stockpile management. The AEC-AFSWP arrangement created 13 AEC-controlled nuclear weapons storage facilities of two different types. Six sites, designated National Stockpile Sites (NSS), held nuclear material while the remaining seven Operational Storage Sites (OSS) performed storage and maintenance. Five of the OSS locations were adjacent to Air Force bases to facilitate rapid loading of nuclear munitions onto waiting aircraft.

In 1950, the USAF began construction on a new and extremely secret installation located near Ellsworth. Known as Rushmore Air Force Station (AFS), the site maintained nuclear munitions for possible use by the heavy bombers stationed at Ellsworth. While an expensive and highly publicized construction program took place at Ellsworth, construction at Rushmore AFS added buildings under a tight veil of secrecy. The construction firm Black and Veatch of Kansas City, Missouri, designed and built facilities at Rushmore and other AEC installations across the country. This secretive mission required administration and operations independent from those at Ellsworth, including separate housing, warehouses, and shop facilities for the Air Force and AEC personnel and their families.

Rushmore AFS did not allow SAC personnel from Ellsworth inside its perimeter due to the secrecy of operations. Air Police at Rushmore AFS provided security for weapons transport, accompanying nuclear weapons leaving the facility for delivery to SAC personnel loading weapons onto waiting bombers. A nearby railhead allowed transport of materiel to and from Rushmore AFS facilities.

Gradually, the military attained increasing responsibility over the nuclear and non-nuclear components, and in the mid-1950s, civilian oversight began to decrease. By 1962, there were no AEC personnel remaining, and Rushmore AFS merged with Ellsworth, becoming the base's Weapon Storage Area (WSA). The end of the Cold War forced Ellsworth's mission refocus in 1991, ending the storage of nuclear weapons on base.

AERIAL REFUELING OVER THE BADLANDS

Many intercontinental bombers had the capability to depart northern air bases in the United States and fly over the North Pole to the Soviet Union. Their internal fuel loads, however, did not always account for any disruptions in the flight plan. SAC bases during the B-52-era included at least one squadron of KC-135 Stratotankers equipped for aerial refueling of the bomber force. The 28 BMW had three aerial refueling squadrons attached over the decades:

28th Air Refueling Squadron (October 1960 to September 1991)
97th Air Refueling Squadron (July 1962 to March 1964)
928th Air Refueling Squadron (February 1959 to October 1960)

POST-ATTACK COMMAND AND CONTROL SYSTEM

Ellsworth's KC-135 fleet also occupied a unique position within the USAF. With over 225 hand-picked officers and enlisted personnel, the 4th Airborne Command and Control Squadron (4 ACCS) was assigned the Post Attack Command and Control System (PACCS) mission of maintaining communications between the national command authority and worldwide nuclear combat forces. The 4 ACCS contained a formal Air Force training school for Airborne Launch Control System (ALCS) Operational Readiness Training (ORT), instructing personnel at other Command and Control squadrons flying the ALCS mission. All EC-135 aircraft flown by the squadron were both refueler and receiver capable—able to pass and receive fuel—requiring 4 ACCS aircrews to be both tanker and receiver qualified. The ALCS mission gave the capability of launching all 1,000 Minuteman intercontinental ballistic missiles (ICBMs) (later, 950 Minuteman and 50 Peacekeeper missiles).

In addition to its alert commitments, the squadron also flew test and training missions: higher headquarters PACCS exercises, trailing wire antenna missions, communications training exercises, combat crew training missions, simulated electronic launch-Minuteman (SELM) and -Peacekeeper (SELP) tests, and operational test launches (GLORY TRIPS) from Vandenberg AFB, California.

THE SHOWPLACE OF SAC

Throughout the 1960s and 1970s, Ellsworth's combination of heavy bombardment aircraft and missile operations made the base the premier installation of SAC, earning the nickname, "The Showplace of SAC." Staffing at the base exceeded 6,000 personnel throughout these decades, and numerous physical improvements took place. Among the projects were several runway and airfield upgrades, additional family housing developments, and new shopping, recreational, and civic buildings for the residential area. Other construction projects continued into the 1980s, allowing the base to demolish remaining World War II–era buildings. Significant changes came to Ellsworth in 1986, starting with the departure of the last B-52 bombers. Ellsworth prepared for the arrival of a new generation of heavy bombardment aircraft, the B-1B Lancer (although aircrews prefer the nickname "Bone," after its spelled-out designation, "B-ONE"). The first of the sleek new aircraft arrived in South Dakota in January 1987.

The B-1Bs took over where the B-52s had left off, serving as strategic nuclear bombardment aircraft. Although considered by some American military planners to be trouble-prone, the B-1Bs at Ellsworth have proved themselves an effective and reliable component of the USAF's bomber fleet. Operations at Ellsworth changed even more dramatically in 1991, as long-standing Cold War tensions began to thaw. The base's nuclear ordnance was removed that year, and replaced with conventional bombs. A far more significant change to the base, however, was the 1991 presidential decision to deactivate all of Ellsworth's LGM-30F Minuteman II missiles. The former missile sites were systematically destroyed, although two facilities were preserved for use as Cold War interpretive sites, the National Park Service's Minuteman Missile National Historic Site. Dismantling Ellsworth's missile infrastructure began immediately and was complete by July 5, 1994, with the inactivation of the 44th Missile Wing.

This aerial view of Rapid City, South Dakota, in 1942 mirrors many other cities and towns across the United States, showing people and technological progress. When the Japanese attacked Pearl Harbor on December 7, 1941, they woke a sleeping economic and military juggernaut that would strike the decisive blow against the Empire of the Rising Sun in 1945. (28th Bomb Wing History Office.)

One

RAPID CITY ARMY AIR BASE

1942–1947

The construction of RCAAB took place from April to September 1942, with the United Construction Company, a consortium of small Rapid City–based contractors, completing building construction, while the Northwest Engineering Company (also from Rapid City) built the runways and utilities. The US Army Corps of Engineers transferred the first completed buildings to the US Army Air Forces' Second Air Force on July 31, 1942, signifying the base's official activation.

The 96th Bombardment Group was the first organization to train at RCAAB, even before construction was complete. The first of the group's seven B-17 Flying Fortresses touched down on September 29, 1942, marking the first official aircraft landing at the base. The base instructed B-17 bomber crew trainees on all phases of flight. This was no small feat, since a B-17 crew had 10 positions: pilot, copilot, navigator, radioman, flight engineer, bombardier, and four machine gunners throughout the aircraft.

Between September 1942 and June 1943, nine heavy bombardment groups and ten provisional groups completed their B-17 training at RCAAB. In July 1943, the base officially activated the combat crew training school, moving the training focus from large echelons (groups/squadrons) to individual aircrews. Germany's surrender to Allied forces on May 7, 1945, was the denouement of the steadily declining need for replacement B-17 crews. US Army Air Forces (USAAF) officials readied the base for closure, placing it on standby status on July 15, 1945. Political pressure forced a reversal, and RCAAB returned to active status over a week later. The revival also brought a new training mission for weather reconnaissance flights using the P-61 Black Widow. This mission lasted until May 1946, when the USAAF reorganized for its postwar future.

DECEMBER 15, 1941.

Special Promotion Piece Issued By

THE RAPID CITY DAILY JOURNAL

"The Newspaper of Western South Dakota"

ASSOCIATED PRESS LEASED WIRE

RAPID CITY, SOUTH DAKOTA

Rapid City, S. D., Named Site $8,500,000 Army Air Base; Bomb Range Near Badlands

Rapid City, S. D.—Associated Press

Contracts are expected to be let within a month for the construction of an $8,500,000 army air base for the training of bomber pilots and bombardiers near Rapid City.

Announcement that Rapid City has been selected for one of seven such schools in the United States, with a personnel of 4,000 men or over, was made in Washington Wednesday morning.

The plant, with the local municipal airport as a nucleus, will cover 1,440 acres, in addition to a 750-square-mile gunnery range and bombing field south of the Badlands national monument. It will have an annual payroll of approximately $2,000,000.

The base is expected to be permanent.

In Strato Area

The sites are within 20 miles of the site of the army air corps stratosphere flights of a few years ago, culminating in the world record flight on Armistice day, 1935, from the Strato bowl, 11 miles from Ra-

project, as far as Rapid City was concerned, has been "up in the air."

Congressmen Help

All of South Dakota's congressional delegation has been active in trying to bring the base to South Dakota. Congressman Francis Case, Custer, has been particularly active on behalf of Rapid City. Senator Chan Gurney, Yankton, and Senator William Bulow, Beresford, also worked hard on the project and lent all assistance possible to all prospective cities, as did Congressman Karl Mundt, Madison.

Rapid City is "traveling in fast company" in being selected as one of the seven sites. Populations of the other six range from about 20,000 to over 300,000 population.

They compare as follows:

	1930	1940
Rapid City	10,404	13,848
Walla Walla	15,976	18,104
Greenville	29,154	34,734
Nashville	153,866	167,402
Richmond	182,929	193,041
Syracuse	209,326	205,967
Columbus	290,564	306,087

army in establishing its base.

"Patriotic Duty"

"This is a big thing for Rapid City", members of the commission said, "with many benefits accruing from it; but even if it wasn't, even if Rapid City wasn't to get back a cent, as a patriotic duty in line of national defense we would do it anyway."

Some of the benefits immediately evident were pointed out as increased population, a permanent "indus-

try" with a payroll of about $2,000,000 per year, a greatly improved airport that will allow commercial aviation development and others.

5,000 MEN TO BE STATIONED HERE

The personnel of the Rapid City bombing base will probably be nearer 5,000 men than the 4,000 men announced Wednesday, according to a telegram received here Thursday from Congressman Francis Case, in Washington.

Plans as laid out at the present time include 450 officers and 4,500 men, Case wired.

About 130 planes of the medium bombardment type are to be used in training, he added.

Case's explanation on finances indicates that construction of buildings and other facilities of that type at the local field will cost $7,500,000, the other $1,000,000 to include securing land, paving runways and aprons and otherwise developing the field itself and the target range of 750 square miles. The target range is to be located south of the Bad Lands national monument.

New details of construction include 250 units, made up of 60 en-

listed men's barracks, 6 mess buildings, bachelor quarters for 400 officers 2 or 3 hangars 120 feet by 200 feet and four concrete runways, 150 feet by 6,000 feet.

Other developments contingent to the air base are also expected, but are not definite as yet. Gas and power expansions are already promised. Railroad facilities for materials are being considered, as are huge supply depots for gasoline and other needed materials.

HILLS AIRPORTS MAY BE AIDED

Washington, Dec. 11—(AP)—Possibility of developing supporting fields at neighboring communities in connection with the new army air base at Rapid City, S. Dak., was seen today by Representative Case (R-SD).

"If the target range is developed then it in all probability will mean some improvement of airports at Spearfish, Hot Springs, Philip and possibly one other point as supporting fields for the Rapid City base."

Case Predicts Fall River Will Get $15,000,000

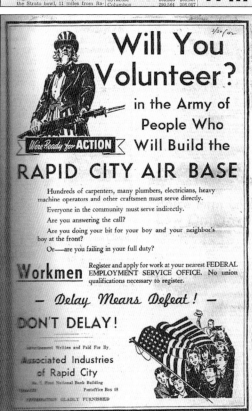

Will You Volunteer?

in the Army of People Who Will Build the

RAPID CITY AIR BASE

We're Ready for ACTION

Hundreds of carpenters, many plumbers, electricians, heavy machine operators and other craftsmen must serve directly.

Everyone in the community must serve indirectly.

Are you answering the call?

Are you doing your bit for your boy and your neighbor's boy at the front?

Or——are you failing in your full duty?

Workmen Register and apply for work at your nearest FEDERAL EMPLOYMENT SERVICE OFFICE. No union qualifications necessary to register.

— *Delay Means Defeat!* —

DON'T DELAY!

Advertisement Written and Paid For By

Associated Industries of Rapid City

First National Bank Building

Postoffice Box 48

Information GLADLY FURNISHED

The December 15, 1941, *Rapid City Daily Journal* announced the Army's decision to build an air base in western South Dakota. The construction estimate was $8.5 million ($149 million in 2020 dollars), with over $1 million earmarked for securing land, paving runways, and developing the field and nearby target range. (28th Bomb Wing History Office.)

This advertisement from the Associated Industries of Rapid City pulled on the patriotic heartstrings of locals during a recruitment drive in March 1942. Jingoistic lines such as "Are you answering the call?" and "Are you failing in your full duty?" attempted to persuade potential workers to support the war effort by building the base, and lining the coffers of the businesses on contract. (28th Bomb Wing History Office.)

Two sentries flank the Rapid City Army Air Base main gate, while a military policeman sits in his Ford four-wheel-drive GPW vehicle, colloquially known as a "jeep." The combat crew training school taught thousands of men from nine heavy bombardment groups from September 1942 through July 1945. Incidentally, the noticeable difference between a Ford Jeep and one produced by Willys-Overland is the nine-slot grille. Willys had seven slots. (28th Bomb Wing History Office.)

Boeing B-17 Flying Fortresses hold formation while flying over Rapid City. Formation flying like this provided the best means of defense for bomber aircraft groups against German fighters. Aerial gunners provided cover for both their aircraft and others within the formation. (28th Bomb Wing History Office.)

These aerial photographs of RCAAB, taken around 1942, show the main runway, hangar facilities, and other garrison buildings. The image above, looking southwest, shows the parking ramp filled with B-17 Flying Fortresses and one formation preparing for takeoff on the far runway. The image below shows a high oblique view of the far east side of RCAAB. The aforementioned runway is at the top. (Both, 28th Bomb Wing History Office.)

Wartime buildings, such as the barracks seen above, were constructed in a short time during the base's early days. Considered temporary garrisons, wartime training airbases had little need for paved roads and sidewalks. South Dakota's inclement weather, however, usually turned these makeshift streets into mud. Below, a General Motors 2.5-ton tactical truck, best known as a "jimmy" or "deuce and a half," drives along a muddy avenue on base. (Both, 28th Bomb Wing History Office.)

A B-17 Flying Fortress sits on the RCAAB parking ramp amid significant snowfall. Echoes of this scene would appear in subsequent decades, with other bomber aircraft waiting patiently in the South Dakota snowfall. (28th Bomb Wing History Office.)

A B-18 Bolo taxies to the runway for another training mission. Considered underpowered and too small to carry a bombload for decisive combat action, the B-18 was plentiful in the pre–World War II US Army Air Corps. However, by 1942, most B-18s flew training missions to help new bombardiers hit their mark. (28th Bomb Wing History Office.)

A snowblower moves the powder away from a B-17 Flying Fortress undergoing maintenance. While the winter climate at Rapid City was typically worse than the weather in the European theater of operations, maintenance crews at RCAAB proved their ability to operate in the harshest circumstances. (28th Bomb Wing History Office.)

Aircrew trainees inspect the No. 2 engine propeller on a B-17 Flying Fortress on a snow-covered flight line. Preflight inspection before takeoff provided opportunities for crews to identify any possible problems before going airborne. The preflight walk-around also permitted maintenance personnel to gently remind aircrews that the aircraft "belongs" to them and should be brought back home in one piece. (28th Bomb Wing History Office.)

A radio transmitter set sits in the RCAAB air traffic control tower around 1944. This radio receiver was the primary link between the ground and the numerous aircraft flying overhead. All bomber crews trained on techniques for landing amidst silence caused by radio failure. However, nothing compared to the welcoming voice of the air traffic controller providing landing instructions at the crew's home airfield. (28th Bomb Wing History Office.)

B-17 Flying Fortresses line the parking ramp on a sunny day in 1942. Note the distance from the air traffic control tower and base operations (far right) to the aircraft (far left). Present-day aircrews have farther to travel, with many aircraft parking spots located away from base ops for safety and security. (28th Bomb Wing History Office.)

Bob Hope (1903–2003) and his entourage brought his comedy to the troops of Rapid City Army Air Base during World War II. Born in London, England, Hope started his show business career in the 1920s. Between 1941 and 1991, Hope headlined 57 USO tours entertaining US troops around the world. In 1997, the US Congress passed a bill that made Hope an honorary veteran of the US armed forces. (28th Bomb Wing History Office.)

Three aircrew members, wearing leather jackets with fur collars, walk along a dirt path at RCAAB in June 1944. The temperatures experienced by B-17 crewmembers at mission altitude (25,000–30,000 feet) could be as low as minus-60 degrees Fahrenheit, making the jackets necessary for survival. (28th Bomb Wing History Office.)

RCAAB trainees shop at the base's post exchange while chatting with Ellouise Opdycke. The "PX," as it was commonly known, provided services and basic personal items to military members, ranging from postcards to soda pop. (28th Bomb Wing History Office.)

The RCAAB's very high frequency (VHF) antenna holds a prominent position near the airfield's runway. While pilots and bombardiers practiced flying and dropping bombs, airborne radio operators learned how to navigate via a variety of techniques, from celestial to radio navigation and voice direction. (28th Bomb Wing History Office.)

Two

GUARDIAN OF THE NORTH
1948–1965

In March 1946, the USAAF split its responsibilities into three commands: Tactical Air Command, responsible for support to ground and naval troops; Air Defense Command, responsible for aerial protection of the United States; and Strategic Air Command, which led planning and execution of strategic, long-range air combat. SAC gained RCAAB as an operating base, and on March 23, 1947, the USAAF reactivated the 28th Bombardment Group (28 BG) at RCAAB. The group consisted of three bomb squadrons of the venerable B-29 Superfortress, the largest of the World War II–era bombers. On September 18, 1947, the USAAF became a separate military service, the USAF.

The Superfortresses did not remain in South Dakota long. By May 1949, Convair's B-36 Peacemaker replaced the 28 BG's B-29s. The B-36 was SAC's first bomber designed from the start to carry nuclear weapons to intercontinental targets. The basing of a large fleet of atomic bombers in South Dakota required a nearby stockpile location for armament. In 1952, construction commenced on Rushmore AFS, an AEC depot and operational storage site for atomic and thermonuclear weapons.

An aircraft tragedy in 1953 gave the base its current name, honoring the 28th Strategic Reconnaissance Wing's commander at the time, Brig. Gen. Richard E. Ellsworth. The mid-1950s saw a transition away from propeller-driven bombers toward an all-jet fleet. The Air Force's first all-jet intercontinental bomber, the Boeing B-52 Stratofortress, paired with the KC-135's aerial refueling capability, gave Ellsworth aircrews the ability to strike targets anywhere in the world.

Officials gather to recognize the naming of Rapid City Air Force Base on June 24, 1948. After the birth of the US Air Force on September 18, 1947, the airbase remained Rapid City Air Field until January 13, 1948, when Air Force chief of staff Carl A. Spaatz renamed the location Weaver Air Force Base after Major General Walter R. Weaver (1885–1944). Public outcry saw the base renamed Rapid City Air Force Base only six months later. (28th Bomb Wing History Office.)

A Boeing B-29 (serial No. 45-21733) belonging to the 717th Bombardment Squadron (717 BS) sits on the flight line at Elmendorf Field around 1946–1947. The 717 BS was one of two bomb squadrons within the 28 BG that moved from Nebraska to Alaska before settling in Rapid City in April 1947. (28th Bomb Wing History Office.)

A Boeing B-29 Superfortress approaches the RCAAB runway. While touted as the best American bomber of World War II, the grim joke among B-29 crewmen was that more of them were killed by Curtiss-Wright, the makers of the B-29's big radial engines, than by Japanese fighters. This reputation did not readily improve after the war. (28th Bomb Wing History Office.)

This B-29 (serial No. 44-84088) at RAF Scampton (1948) sports the 6th Bombardment Group's pirate logo near the cockpit and the distinctive circle-R tail insignia. It is likely the 6 BG transferred its B-29s to the newly activated 28 BG before inactivating in late 1948. B-29 aircraft transfer records are spotty, but there is overwhelming photographic evidence of circle-R B-29s at RCAFB to support this hypothesis. (28th Bomb Wing History Office.)

After initiation of the Berlin Blockade in June 1948, the 28 BG at RCAFB was placed on 12-hour alert status for immediate deployment to Europe. In late July, the 28 BG flew to RAF Scampton. The 28 BG consisted of conventionally armed B-29s, as the bulk of the atomic bombardment force resided at other air bases in the United States. (28th Bomb Wing History Office.)

Snow covers B-29s on RCAFB's flight line in early 1948. Note the maintenance scaffolds covered in snow, illustrating snow removal had not taken place at the time of the photograph. (28th Bomb Wing History Office.)

Boeing B-29 (serial No. 44-84078) shows off its distinct circle-R insignia and buzz number in this undated photograph. The circle-R tail belonged to the 6th Bombardment Group during World War II and was famously used by the B-29 *Enola Gay* to conceal its true origins. B-29 serial No. 44-84078 would later be converted into a SB-29 "Super Dumbo" air-sea rescue craft in 1950. (28th Bomb Wing History Office.)

The 612th USAF Band poses at RCAFB around 1952. Historically, musicians provided tempo for marching military troops; the modern band's existence is owed to esprit de corps and camaraderie. Bands such as this provide music during official presentations, such as funerals and distinguished visits, and musical shows for the public. (28th Bomb Wing History Office.)

Fire crews practice response actions during training in mid-1954. Air crash rates from the early days of the Cold War necessitated rapid fire response near the runways and flight line. (28th Bomb Wing History Office.)

The 54th Fighter Interceptor Squadron (54 FIS) operated from RCAFB from December 1952 through December 1960. Its mission was to provide air defense for the north central United States, which held the core of atomic (and later thermonuclear) deterrence forces throughout the Cold War. (28th Bomb Wing History Office.)

The 54 FIS flew F-89 Scorpions from Ellsworth AFB from 1957 until its inactivation in 1960. The F-89 was one of the first Air Force fighters equipped with guided missiles and was the first combat aircraft armed with air-to-air nuclear weapons, the AIR-2 Genie rocket. The Genie gave the F-89 the ability to destroy approaching bomber formations with an atomic airburst. (28th Bomb Wing History Office.)

This undated image shows the comparative sizes of SAC's bomber force in the late 1940s and early 1950s. Clockwise from the right are a B-36 Peacemaker, B-17 Flying Fortress, B-29 Superfortress, and B-23 Dragon. Personnel at RCAFB flew each of these bombers (minus the B-23) at some point in the base's early history. The B-23 Dragon was the redesigned successor to the B-18 Bolo, which trained aircrews at RCAAB. (US Air Force.)

B-36s lumber along the runway at Rapid City Air Force Base in the early 1950s. SAC introduced the jet-and-propeller driven aircraft into the inventory as a "very heavy bomber" in late 1948. Simultaneously, SAC reclassified the still-operational B-29 and B-50 Superfortresses as medium, rather than heavy, bombers. (US Air Force.)

The Mark 17 thermonuclear bomb entered service in 1954 and served until 1957 as the first mass-produced hydrogen (thermonuclear) bomb in the US inventory. Only the B-36 could carry the Mark 17, with the bomb taking up the aircraft's two aft bomb bays, while the forward bomb bay held a Mark 6 atomic bomb. Rushmore AFS stored a stockpile of Mark 17s for Ellsworth's B-36 fleet. (National Archives.)

The K-42 Camera Model, also known as the "Boston camera," was the largest aerial camera ever built. It was test-flown on an RB-36 in 1954, but was not introduced into the force. RB-36 photoreconnaissance aircraft had 14 to 23 different cameras, along with an onboard darkroom to develop photographs while in flight. (National Museum of the US Air Force.)

B-36s are scattered around the RCAFB flight line in the early 1950s. One B-36 (center) is undergoing inspection, with its wings covered by the No. 5 maintenance dock. (28th Bomb Wing History Office.)

Maintenance is performed on a pair of J47-GE-19 jet engines inside a shelter pod. The size of the aircraft, along with the limited hangar facilities, saw many hours of outdoor flight line maintenance in both sun and snow. (28th Bomb Wing History Office.)

The vertical stabilizer (tail) of a B-36 pokes out from a maintenance hangar. The B-36 had a 230-foot wingspan and 162-foot length, with a towering 46-foot vertical stabilizer, so specialized facilities were needed for repairs and periodic maintenance. (28th Bomb Wing History Office.)

Three Pratt & Whitney R-4360-53 Wasp Major propeller engines are seen inside a maintenance hangar. As the only US bomber using both jet and propeller technology, the B-36 was a transition aircraft, bringing the US bomber force into the jet age. The aircraft's unofficial slogan was "six turning, four burning." (28th Bomb Wing History Office.)

Seen above is an artist's conception of the "very, very heavy bomber" (VVHB) hangar designed to house the B-36 Peacemaker. The B-36 hangar was initially developed in mid-1947 by the engineering firm of Roberts & Schaefer of Chicago as a monolithic, rib-and-shell vault structure designed to accommodate two B-36s. Below, construction trusses support the roof structure. Only three hangars of this type are known to have been constructed—one at Ellsworth (Pride Hangar); one at Loring AFB, Maine (Arch Hangar); and one at Travis AFB, California. (Both, 28th Bomb Wing History Office.)

The VVHB hangar, under early construction at RCAFB, shows only three ribbed cantilevers completed. (28th Bomb Wing History Office.)

A B-36 rolls next to the completed VVHB hangar in the early 1950s. Bomber designations after World War II briefly saw the B-29, and its updated version the B-50, designated a "very heavy bomber," while the Convair B-36 was debuted as a "very, very heavy bomber." (28th Bomb Wing History Office.)

The American flag flies over the headquarters of the 3081st Aviation Depot Squadron at Rushmore AFS. The classified atomic munitions depots were built by the Kansas City engineering firm of Black & Veatch. The first four atomic-storage "Q Areas" were all national sites operated by the AEC. By the mid-1950s, 20 Q-Areas existed around the world, including one at Rushmore AFS. (28th Bomb Wing History Office.)

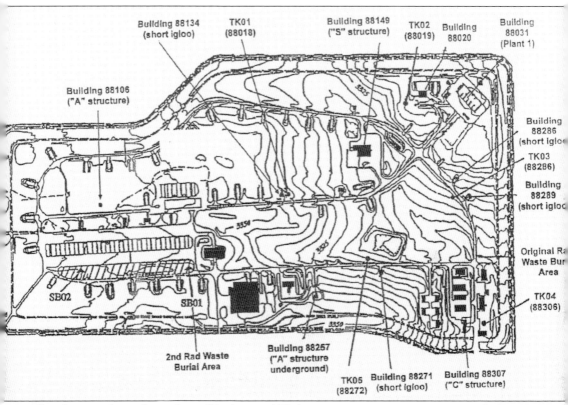

Building 88134
(short igloo)

TK01
(88018)

Building 88149
("S" structure)

TK02
(88019)

Building
88020

Building
88031
(Plant 1)

Building 88106
("A" structure)

Building
88286
(short igloo)

TK03
(88286)

Building
88289
(short igloo)

Original Ra
Waste Bur
Area

TK04
(88306)

SB02

SB01

2nd Rad Waste
Burial Area

Building 88257
("A" structure
underground)

TK06
(88272)

Building 88271
(short igloo)

Building 88307
("C" structure)

This diagram shows the outline of Rushmore AFS during its time as an atomic storage Q Area. Many of the buildings have been demolished to make way for newer storage igloos for Ellsworth's conventional weapons. The distinct outline of the station can be seen on satellite imagery even today. (Sandia National Laboratories.)

Richard Elmer Ellsworth (1911–1953) was born in Erie, Pennsylvania, and served in the Pennsylvania National Guard for two years before entering the US Military Academy in 1931. He attended pilot training at Randolph and Kelly Fields, Texas. After a distinguished career in a variety of staff jobs, Ellsworth was promoted to brigadier general in September 1952 at RCAFB, where he was wing commander of the 28th Strategic Reconnaissance Wing. (US Air Force.)

The wreckage of RB-36H (serial No. 51-13721) rests on a hill outside Burgoynes Cove, Newfoundland. On March 17, 1953, General Ellsworth's RB-36 took off from the Canary Islands on a mission to test US air defenses. During the early morning of March 18, his B-36 crashed into a mountain during low-level flight, killing all 23 crew members aboard. (HiddenNewfoundland.ca.)

On June 13, 1953, Pres. Dwight D. Eisenhower visited RCAFB to rename the air base in memory of Brigadier General Ellsworth. (28th Bomb Wing History Office.)

Ellsworth's final resting place is among other fallen warriors within the Black Hills National Cemetery, near Sturgis, South Dakota. (28th Bomb Wing Public Affairs Office.)

The base hospital is seen under construction in the early 1950s. After being declared a permanent installation, as opposed to its "temporary" wartime status nearly a decade prior, Ellsworth AFB began receiving funds for modernized facilities for the military members and their families during the early days of the Cold War. (28th Bomb Wing History Office.)

The iconic B-36 hangar houses aircraft for public viewing during an air show in the mid-1950s. This facility would later house the headquarters of the 44th Strategic Missile Wing (44 SMW) and its associated squadrons during the Minuteman missile buildup of the early 1960s. (28th Bomb Wing History Office.)

Three

STRATEGIC MODERNIZATION IN THE BADLANDS
1966–1991

In 1965, the 28 BMW received EC-135 aircraft to support the Post-Attack Command and Control System (PACCS) airborne command post mission of SAC. The EC-135 was specially equipped with VHF radio and multiplex equipment, which was designed to allow SAC's commander to continue communications during a nuclear attack. In the late 1960s, the 44 SMW was responsible for testing and development of the Airborne Launch Control System (ALCS) that would link the PACCS aircraft to the Minuteman ICBMs. The 44 SMW had ALCS responsibility for Minot AFB and Grand Forks AFB, North Dakota; Malmstrom AFB, Montana; F.E. Warren AFB, Wyoming; and Ellsworth AFB. In April 1970, the ALCS was combined with the PACCS and the Western Auxiliary Command Post, forming the 4th Airborne Command and Control Squadron (4 ACCS), which was then assigned to the 28 BMW.

In 1966, the first Ellsworth AFB B-52 bombers were sent to Vietnam and the 28 BMW continued involvement until the United States withdrew from the war. In 1986, the 28 BMW began to phase out the B-52s and prepared to become the home for the B-1B Lancer. The preparation for the B-1B included upgrading the runway and constructing new dormitories. In 1991, the 28 BMW was redesignated the 28th Wing (28 WG). The designation did not last long, however. On June 1, 1992, SAC was inactivated; the 28 WG was redesignated the 28th Bomb Wing (28 BW) and Ellsworth was reassigned to Air Combat Command. The mission of the 28 BW changed from strategic (nuclear) bombardment to worldwide conventional munitions delivery.

The first B-52D (serial No. 56-0657) at Ellsworth AFB shines in its early–Cold War metallic sheen after its delivery from the Boeing Wichita factory in July 1957. This B-52D was one of 170 "D" model variants and saw combat during the Vietnam War dropping conventional bombs. Used as a "gate guard" for decades, serial No. 56-0657 was later moved to the South Dakota Air and Space Museum outside the Liberty Gate. (28th Bomb Wing History Office.)

A B-52 Stratofortress flies a low-level route over an unidentified Titan I missile site in the early 1960s, showcasing two legs of the strategic triad. (28th Bomb Wing History Office.)

Captain Zellers reviews the times of religious gatherings at the Ellsworth AFB chapel in the early 1960s. Respecting the religious rights of American military personnel, many bases provided ample opportunities for worship, albeit in the same shared facilities. (28th Bomb Wing History Office.)

The headquarters building of the 28th Bombardment Wing (Heavy) shows snowfall. The 28th used the "heavy" descriptor from October 1955 to distinguish from the medium bomb wings flying the B-47 Stratojet and FB-111. Heavy was dropped from the unit's name on September 1, 1991, when the wing was redesignated the 28th Wing. (28th Bomb Wing History Office.)

A B-52G Stratofortress flies over a sign welcoming visitors to Rapid City, "Home of the Black Hills Bandits," of the 28th Bombardment Wing and 44th Strategic Missile Wing. (28th Bomb Wing History Office.)

A security police vehicle is stuck in a snowdrift outside the 44 SMW's Pride Hangar during a blizzard in 1972. (28th Bomb Wing History Office.)

On June 9 and 10, 1972, heavy rains collapsed the nearby Canyon Lake Dam, flooding Rapid Creek and overfilling its banks. The flood, equaling 1 billion metric tons of water, caused 238 deaths and over $165 million (1972) in damage. Here, two Ellsworth airmen move supplies to assist fellow South Dakotans who lost their homes. (28th Bomb Wing History Office.)

Pres. Gerald R. Ford shakes hands with Ellsworth personnel during a trip to South Dakota in August 1976. (28th Bomb Wing History Office.)

A Boeing KC-135A takes off from Ellsworth AFB. Note the midline stripe (left of the US Air Force markings) with the 28 BMW emblem. The base received its first KC-135 Stratotanker refueling aircraft in 1959 to support the deterrence mission of the wing's B-52 bombers. (National Archives.)

The entrance to the 28th Bomb Wing Tanker–PACCS Alert Facility allowed access to a high-security area of the base. Aircrews would remain on alert during designated periods, though the ground alert mission for the KC-135/EC-135s was continual. (National Archives.)

A maintenance member uses a pump to withdraw JP-4 jet fuel from an underground tank to fill a KC-135 Stratotanker. JP-4 was a 50-50 kerosene-gasoline blend and was the primary Air Force jet fuel between 1951 and 1995. (National Archives.)

A staff sergeant speaks to the aircrew while performing preflight inspections on a KC-135 for exercise Global Shield 84. (National Archives.)

Painting aircraft with nose art began in 1913 prior to World War I. During the two major wars of the 20th century, the variety of nose emblems ranged from the simplistic to the near obscene. This SAC KC-135 sports an image of *Orcinus orca*, better known as a killer whale. (National Archives.)

The crew of KC-135A (serial No. 59-1459) knew their place in the SAC pecking order, as shown with this nose art. Aerial refueling crews were often called "tanker toads," dating to the debut of the Stratotanker's service within SAC. TOAD stands for "take off and die," for after their mission of refueling northbound B-52s was complete, tanker crews had no fuel left over to recover at a friendly air base. (National Archives.)

Stratotanker (serial No. 59-1446) shows the Tasmanian Devil character hanging on an aerial refueling boom. While many pieces of artwork are self-explanatory, others are often in-jokes or have relevance to the crew or crew chief who named the aircraft. (National Archives.)

A picturesque view of Mount Rushmore is in the background as KC-135 Stratotanker (serial No. 59-1455) flies past. The monument at Mount Rushmore has provided the backdrop for many aerial photographs as a distinct part of the South Dakota cultural landscape. (National Archives.)

Airman First Class William Haase guards a B-52H Stratofortress aircraft on Ellsworth's flight line during Global Shield 84. This scene was commonplace during the 1970s and 1980s as the Cold War reached a fever pitch. (National Archives.)

Crews rush out of the bomber alert facility, known as the "Mole Hole," toward waiting trucks. Bomber crews sat 24-hour alert during the Cold War, waiting for a klaxon alarm. (National Archives.)

After departing the bomber alert facility, aircrew members rush into vehicles that will transport them to their aircraft on the flight line. As warning times decreased due to the introduction of ICBMs, SAC aircrews had less time to get their aircraft airborne before the impending destruction of their base. (National Archives.)

Here is an aerial view of Ellsworth's alert ramp, also known as the "Christmas tree," due to its unique design. The parking scheme allowed rapid queuing and takeoff of the B-52s, one right after another. (National Archives.)

A 28 BMW B-52 is refueled by a KC-135 Stratotanker. After getting airborne, both aircraft would meet up. KC-135 crews would off-load the majority of its onboard fuel to the B-52s heading over the North Pole. Stratotanker crews would remain at their aerial refueling point until they ran out of fuel over Canada or the Arctic Ocean. (National Archives.)

Using the drogue parachute to slow its velocity, a B-52 lands at Ellsworth (above). In the unlikely scenario any B-52 survived its nuclear strike on the Soviet Union, it would attempt to land at friendly airbases in Europe. Aircraft decontamination (right) was performed by Ellsworth ground crews for Global Shield 84. Surviving B-52s would likely have flown through radioactive clouds on their egress routes, requiring radiological decontamination. (Both, National Archives.)

A munitions handler inspects a B-28FI bomb on a "clip" containing four bombs before installation on a B-52 at Ellsworth AFB on April 1, 1984. The variety of weapons carried by the B-52 over the decades ranged from kiloton to multi-megaton nuclear bombs. Some weapons, like the B-28FI seen here, used unguided delivery methods with a parachute. (National Archives.)

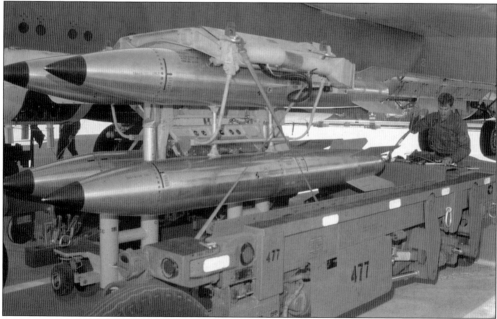

A clip of four B-61 "Dr. Pepper" bombs is moved into position for loading. The B-61 was originally designed during the Kennedy administration but has remained in service, with 13 modifications over the decades. Its unique "dial-a-yield" characteristics offered flexibility to nuclear war planners on desired blast yields. (National Archives.)

Members of the 319th Bombardment Wing from Grand Forks AFB, North Dakota, load AGM-86 air-launched cruise missiles (ALCMs) onto a B-52 during the 1985 SAC Combat Weapons Loading Competition at Ellsworth. ALCMs gave the B-52 a standoff capability, allowing the aircraft to remain outside hostile airspace while launching its missiles at their targets. (National Archives.)

A crew readies a B-52 with AGM-69 short-range attack missiles (SRAM) (top) and a clip of four B-28 gravity bombs. SRAMs provided a standoff capability for the increasingly vulnerable B-52. The missiles were coated in rubber to dissipate heat during their rapid launch, being nicknamed "Nerf missiles" by crews after the popular foam toy. (National Archives.)

The last B-52H departs Ellsworth AFB in March 1986 for a final flight over Rapid City. The 28 BMW's B-52Hs were consolidated at other bases to make room for SAC's newest bomber, the B-1B. (National Archives.)

A sign proudly proclaims the base as "Black Hills Bandit territory" around 1986. The Black Hills Bandit mascot originates from seven stagecoach robberies near Deadwood, South Dakota, in 1876–1877. The six bandits later turned to train robberies. (National Archives.)

The first B-1B bomber (serial No. 85-0073) arrives at Ellsworth AFB on January 21, 1987. The aircraft was dubbed "the Wings of Freedom" and was flown by the commander-in-chief of Strategic Air Command, Gen. John T. Chain Jr. (US Air Force.)

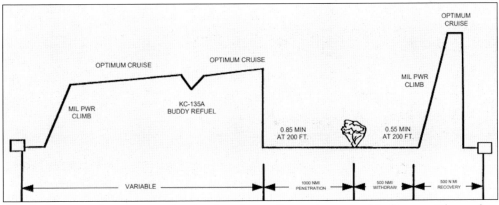

The B-1B's original mission was low-level nuclear strike, as shown in this diagram. The nuclear delivery mission only lasted a handful of years before the end of the Cold War. (National Archives.)

Sgt. Lee E. DuBry (left), 28th Munitions Maintenance Squadron, inspects BDU-38 practice shapes (representing B-61 Dr. Pepper bombs) on a B-1B's rotary launcher. The B-1B used a rotary launch system to provide optimal space for weapons inside its two weapons bays. Below, members of the 28th Munitions Maintenance Squadron bolt a BDU-38 practice bomb during exercise Proud Shield 88. (Both, National Archives.)

Here, a military formation stands in front of a B-1B around 1990. The B-1B's variable-sweep wings are fully extended. (National Archives.)

Here is Ellsworth AFB's main gate in June 1983. (National Archives.)

Nose art for 28 BW B-1B *Pandora's Box*, pictured around 1988, depicts a female warrior, which would have been considered risqué only a few years before. (National Archives.)

Another 28 BW B-1B, *Spectre*, alludes to the nature of the bomber aircraft to drop ordnance and take lives. (National Archives.)

B-1B *Enforcer* shows a sheriff's badge and a six-shooter pistol, echoing Rapid City's storied history in the Old West. (National Archives.)

B-1B *Mystique* is part of a long tradition of naming aircraft for women, whether real or fantasy. (National Archives.)

Pres. Ronald Reagan waves to the crowd at Ellsworth AFB during a visit to Rapid City on October 29, 1986. Reagan campaigned for Sen. James Abdnor as part of a seven-state tour. Before landing, Air Force One flew past Mount Rushmore twice. (National Archives.)

Special Air Mission (SAM) 29000, commonly known as Air Force One when the president of the United States is aboard, flies over Mount Rushmore on November 11, 1990. Ellsworth AFB is the nearest Air Force installation equipped to support large aircraft such as the VC-25A (a modified Boeing 747). (National Archives.)

In 1988, Adm. William Crowe, chairman of the joint chiefs of staff, pictured above at center, speaks to First Lt. Jill Nagel (far left) during a visit with his Soviet counterpart Marshal Sergei F. Akhromeyev (second from right) on a US-wide tour of military installations to garner support for arms control efforts. Below, Admiral Crowe (far right) smiles next to three 44 SMW personnel in the missile procedures trainer. The missile combat crew members show Marshal Akhromeyev, pictured below second from left, the nuclear deterrence capability represented by the Minuteman II weapon system. (Both, National Archives.)

Members of Team Ellsworth pose after winning the 1990 John L. Hennessy award. Established in 1957, the award is the highest honor an Air Force dining facility can attain. It was named for John L. Hennessy, a hotel and restaurant executive who led an advisory group responsible for improving military food service. (National Archives.)

Ellsworth AFB's trifecta of aircraft fly over Mount Rushmore for an aerial photograph. The B-1B (bottom center) flanks a KC-135 (left) and an EC-135 ALCC. (National Archives.)

A 28 BW KC-135 (right) refuels an EC-135 ALCC over the Badlands. While the EC-135's primary mission was as an airborne launch control center, it maintained the ability to provide in-flight air refueling when necessary. (National Archives.)

A B-1B flies over the "Christmas tree" alert parking ramp, with a B-1B and two EC-135s parked below. (National Archives.)

A KC-135 Stratotanker refuels a B-1B, providing aerial refueling for combat operations. After the introduction of aerial refueling in the late 1940s, SAC truly became a global force with the ability to fly anywhere in the world, drop its munitions, and return to home station without landing. The KC-135 fleet became a force multiplier for SAC's nuclear deterrent. (National Archives.)

Crew chiefs from the 28th Organizational Maintenance Squadron sit inside their vehicle, known as a "bread truck," during nighttime maintenance ops at Ellsworth AFB. (National Archives.)

B-1Bs sit outside their maintenance docks at Ellsworth AFB around 1988. (National Archives.)

A B-1B belonging to the 28th Bomb Wing flies a low-level route over the Badlands, near a 44 SMW launch control facility (upper left). (National Archives.)

The logo of the 44th (Strategic) Missile Wing shows an AVCO Mark II reentry vehicle pointed downward, with a telltale nuclear symbol around the tip. The wing's motto, "Aggressor Beware," aptly described the unit's strategic deterrent mission operating the Minuteman weapon system. (Air Force Historical Research Agency.)

Four

AGGRESSOR BEWARE
1961–1994

The Air Force selected Ellsworth AFB as the location of the second Minuteman unit (Wing II) soon after the installation of the first wing at Malmstrom AFB, Montana. On October 12, 1960, SAC selected Ellsworth over Minot AFB and Grand Forks AFB, North Dakota, which would later gain their own Minuteman missile wings. Secretary of the Air Force Eugene Zuckert announced Ellsworth's official selection on January 5, 1961. Seven months later, on August 1, 1961, Peter Kiewit Sons' Company (of Omaha, Nebraska) won the Wing II construction contract for the bid price of $56,220,274. Construction on the South Dakota Minuteman complex began on August 21, 1961.

Prior to the Minuteman installation, Ellsworth AFB supported first-generation ICBMs in the form of SM-68A Titan I missiles. Three launch sites belonging to the 850th Strategic Missile Squadron (850 SMS) were located near Wicksville (850-A), Hermosa (850-B), and Sturgis (850-C). Each site contained three underground missile launch facilities, bringing South Dakota's ICBM launch facility tally to nine until the Minuteman came. The 850 SMS was an odd duck, as it belonged organizationally to the 28th Bombardment Wing from 1960 through 1962, when the 44th Strategic Missile Wing activated to support Minuteman operations.

The 44th Strategic Missile Wing activated on January 1, 1962, to operate and manage the 12,600-square-mile missile complex. From April 1963 through September 1991, one hundred and fifty Minuteman missiles stood alert 24 hours a day in geographically separated launch facilities around southwestern South Dakota, operated by 15 launch control centers and 30 missile combat crew members underground.

During early discussions for the Strategic Arms Reduction Treaty (START), forward-thinking planners inserted the request to save one launch control facility and one launch facility for historic preservation. Decision makers selected Delta-01 launch control center (LCC) and Delta-09 launch facility (LF) out of the entire Wing II inventory for preservation by the National Park Service. On November 29, 1999, Congress passed Public Law 106-115, establishing the Minuteman Missile National Historic Site. Visitors today can tour the facilities, viewing the working conditions of missile combat crew members and maintainers and peek down inside the launch tube at D-09 LF, complete with a demilitarized Minuteman II missile.

The 850th Strategic Missile Squadron (850 SMS) operated the SM-68 Titan I missile in western South Dakota from December 1, 1960, through March 25, 1965. The squadron's motto, "Always on Target," was almost laughable with the multi-megaton Mark 4 reentry vehicle. Considered a stop-gap until Minuteman came online, Titan I missiles were phased out by Secretary of Defense Robert McNamara in 1965. (Air Force Historical Research Agency.)

The Titan I launch sites in South Dakota were akin to small underground cities, as seen here. The 850 SMS Titans were deployed in a three-by-three configuration, with a total of nine missiles divided between three sites at Wicksville, Hermosa, and Sturgis. The 850 SMS sites were the first missile squadron subjected to a SAC operational readiness inspection, though they did not pass. The first 850 SMS missiles were removed from alert on January 4, 1965. (Chromehooves.net.)

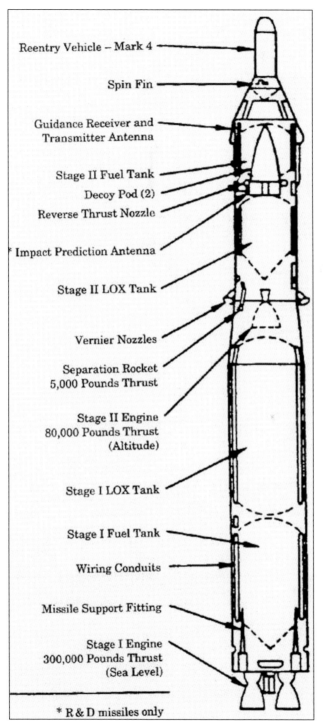

Reentry Vehicle – Mark 4

Spin Fin

Guidance Receiver and
Transmitter Antenna

Stage II Fuel Tank

Decoy Pod (2)

Reverse Thrust Nozzle

* Impact Prediction Antenna

Stage II LOX Tank

Vernier Nozzles

Separation Rocket
5,000 Pounds Thrust

Stage II Engine
80,000 Pounds Thrust
(Altitude)

Stage I LOX Tank

Stage I Fuel Tank

Wiring Conduits

Missile Support Fitting

Stage I Engine
300,000 Pounds Thrust
(Sea Level)

* R & D missiles only

This diagram shows the internal segments that make up the SM-68 Titan I ICBM. Technologies developed for the Titan I program found their way into its successor, the LGM-25C Titan II ICBM, and various space launch vehicles in the Titan family. While its life as a missile was short, Titan space booster variants launched national security satellites until 2005. (US Air Force.)

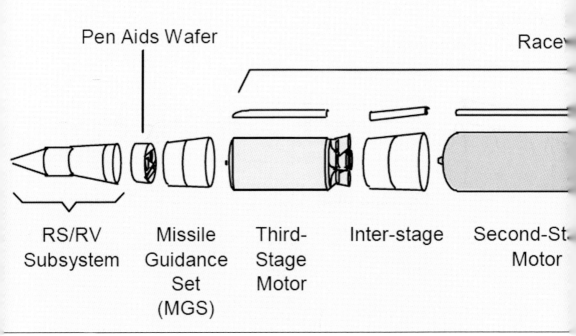

Pen Aids Wafer

Race

RS/RV
Subsystem

Missile
Guidance
Set
(MGS)

Third-
Stage
Motor

Inter-stage

Second-St
Motor

This illustration of an LGM-30F Minuteman II missile shows the three-stage airframe, guidance system, and the reentry vehicle. Many of the downstage rocket motors are nearly identical in length and diameter to LGM-30A/B Minuteman I and LGM-30G Minuteman III missiles used

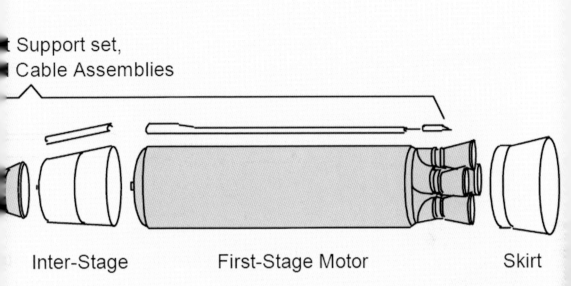

Support set,
Cable Assemblies

Inter-Stage   First-Stage Motor   Skirt

by SAC during the Cold War. Upgrades to propulsion and guidance computers in the early 21st century kept the LGM-30G Minuteman III a viable strategic deterrent long after Ellsworth's Minuteman IIs were retired. (US Air Force.)

Construction begins on an unidentified LCC in South Dakota. The concrete structure (under crane hook) behind the rebar-covered LCC is the elevator shaft, providing access to the facility. As the second Minuteman wing built, Ellsworth facilities did not include the underground equipment building that was present at the later wings in Wyoming, North Dakota, and Missouri. (Library of Congress.)

Steel reinforcing rods surround the acoustical enclosure at an LCC under construction. Reinforced concrete at both the LCC and LF provided the Minuteman weapon system an enhanced survivability rate over the first-generation "soft" Titan and Atlas missiles. (Library of Congress.)

The acoustical enclosure, seen here, housed the missile combat crews and their command-and-control equipment. The box-shaped structure was supported by four shock isolators—acting like large springs—attached to the reinforced concrete "egg." This design planned for near-misses of enemy weapons, allowing the shock isolators to absorb the rocking and rolling from the ground shockwave. The enclosure was also electrically isolated to prevent shorting of equipment by electromagnetic effects caused by nuclear detonations. (National Archives.)

Here is an aerial view of an LCF under construction in South Dakota. The LCC concrete egg is nearly covered with dirt, as the elevator shaft pokes up from the ground. (National Archives.)

A launch tube liner is lifted (above) prior to being placed at an unidentified LF. The launch tube was reinforced with metal to provide increased stability and integrity against nearby nuclear detonations. (Both, National Archives.)

A close-up view of the launch tube liner (above) gives amazing detail to the amount of reinforcement built into the Minuteman LFs. Note the workers atop the structure (top right) for scale. The image below clearly shows the launcher equipment room and personnel access hatch (small circle near center). The Soft Support Building (SSB), to the right of the launch tube, housed power and communication connectivity in a non-reinforced structure. As weapons improved, the survivability probability rates dropped. (Both, National Archives.)

Workers pour concrete into the mold forming the launcher closure door. Weighing around 110 tons, the door protects the missile inside the launch tube against overpressure and thermal blast effects. While extremely heavy, the door opens rapidly due to underground ballistic gas actuators. These armed explosive devices can pull the door open in seconds during a launch. (National Archives.)

A transporter erector positions over the launcher closure door at an unidentified Ellsworth LF. While the ballistic gas actuators provide a rapid-open capability for launch, normal maintenance requires a slower means to "roll the door," as seen by the mechanical device at the door's edge. (National Archives.)

A fully extended transporter erector (TE) shows its immense size, as required by the 57-foot Minuteman II missile. After precise positioning near two fixed pylons by the launcher closure door, the TE is bolted down to minimize movement as the missile downstages are lifted up or down from the launch tube. (National Archives.)

This view looking up from the inside of the LF shows the bottom opening of the TE. Note the "loaded" signage on the second and third stages, indicating the rocket motors are operational, not training devices. (National Archives.)

Another behemoth vehicle in the Air Force inventory is the payload transporter, seen here parked atop a launcher closure door. This truck carries the top of the Minuteman missile: the missile guidance set, the penetration aids wafer, and the reentry vehicle subsystem. After precise positioning straddling the launcher closure door, side panels drop down to protect the warhead and guidance system from the weather. (National Archives.)

Sgt. Russell Taft (left) and Airman First Class David Harris lift a missile guidance set into a maintenance van during Global Shield 84. Note the open hole at the bottom of the vehicle, looking down into the launch tube, necessitating the use of safety harnesses on both personnel. (National Archives.)

Sergeant Taft (left) and Airman First Class Harris inspect a Mark 11 reentry system (covered by a white shroud) mated to its missile guidance set (MGS). A common task in the missile complex is an MGS removal and replacement, requiring the payload transporter to lift the mated systems out of the LF. (National Archives.)

This top-down view of an open LF shows the lowered access door, or "diving board" (center right, obscured by the missile) and the installed work cage (left) containing two people. The upper support ring allows the work cage to rotate 360 degrees around the launch tube, as well as raising and lowering to work on any stage of the Minuteman. (National Archives.)

This unidentified LCF looks like a nondescript "Little House on the Prairie," albeit one surrounded by barbed wire fencing. One hundred of these facilities were spread over the Great Plains at six different missile complexes during the Cold War, during the height of Minuteman's 1,000 missile deployment. (National Archives.)

An airman first class poses in front of an LCF gate. The warning sign, along with the barbed wire fence, gave subtle indications to any wayward visitors to the nondescript compound sitting out on the Great Plains. (National Archives.)

The underground entrance to Delta-01 LCC shows motivational artwork. The pizza box on the blast door was painted by Tony Gatlin in 1989, spoofing a Domino's Pizza advertising slogan of the time. (National Archive.)

The eight-ton LCC blast door provides protection to the missile combat crew from overpressure shockwaves, thermal blast, and saboteurs. The circles along the edge are metal pins that extend to lock the door in place. (National Archives.)

First Lt. Michael Turner (above) and Second Lt. Wesley Collins (below) work inside a Minuteman missile procedures trainer (MPT) during Global Shield 84. The MPT is a simulated LCC. To maintain proficiency, missile combat crew members undertake monthly training "rides" and evaluations inside the aboveground MPT. (Both, National Archives.)

A successful launch takes place at Vandenberg AFB, California. Because Vandenberg is the only operational test launch location for Minuteman missiles, Ellsworth missile combat crew members and maintenance personnel would often travel to California for force development launches, testing technological upgrades and crew training procedures. (National Archives.)

A Boeing EC-135G (serial No. 62-3579) flies over Mount Rushmore on July 6, 1988. The 4 ACCS controlled the Post-Attack Command and Control System mission from Ellsworth AFB. During wartime, Ellsworth's EC-135s (ALCC-1) would orbit between the Minuteman complexes in South Dakota and Francis E. Warren AFB, Wyoming, to the south. (National Archives.)

Aircrew members aboard an EC-135 aircraft monitor information for the SAC battle staff during a flight. If SAC's underground command center were destroyed by enemy attack, the crew of the flying command center would assume all functions from the air. The Looking Glass mission "mirrored" ground facilities in both staff planning, battle space awareness, and launch capability, hence the name. The 4 ACCS infrequently flew Looking Glass missions when Offutt AFB aircrews were unable to. (National Archives.)

The equipment panel pictured above is part of the Common Airborne Launch Control System (CALCS) still in use today, while the image below was part of the Phase II ALCS weapon system retired in 1991. The upgraded CALCS allowed the ALCS to transmit to both Minuteman and Peacekeeper LFs, a capability missing in the earlier system. With the older Phase II system, the commander and deputy launch panels were 12 feet apart and required only two hands (one on each key to launch). The newer CALCS system requires four hands and deliberate motions—two hands twisting keys clockwise and two twisting knobs counterclockwise. Unlike underground LCCs providing one launch vote each, a key turn from the ALCS automatically provides two launch votes, ensuring the missiles will launch without LCC assistance. (Both, National Archives.)

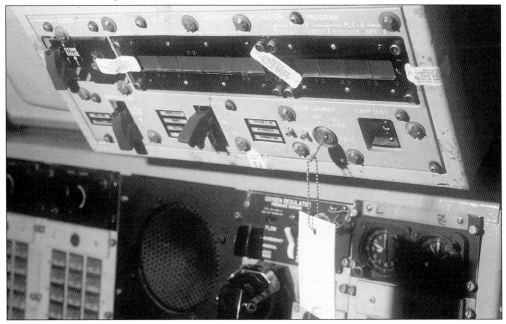

Second Lt. Steven Hughes stands near the open personnel access hatch (PAH) at Lima 05 (L-05). The PAH allowed entry into the launcher equipment room (LER) and access to the missile in the launch tube. The size of the entryway allowed lowering of diagnostic equipment and tools into the LER for maintenance. (John Mills collection, National Park Service.)

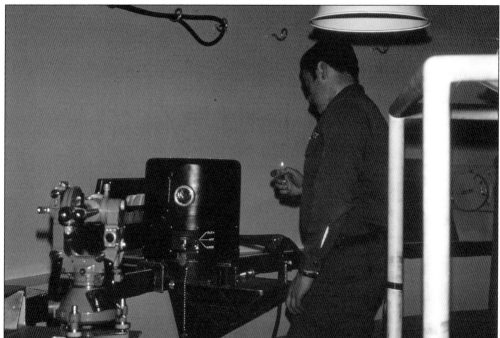

First Lt. Ed Slany operates an azimuth laying set (ALS) inside November 11 (N-11). To accurately target a missile, the system must know where it is, and how it is aligned in the launch tube. The ALS established the azimuth standard in the LF, and combined with an autocollimator and the missile guidance system, proper alignment was obtained. (John Mills collection, National Park Service.)

This view of Charlie 09 (C-09) from an overlooking hill shows the entire LF topside with a maintenance crew and their utility van. The launcher closure door (center) covers the top of the launch tube and protects the Minuteman missile inside. The soft support building (SSB) at far right contains connective equipment for local power. During a nuclear detonation, the SSB and its connection to the outside world would likely be destroyed by blast, overpressure, or debris. (John Mills collection, National Park Service.)

Helicopters, such as this UH-1 Huey, were often used to ferry maintenance personnel, provide overhead route surveys, and provide security during warhead movement. A landing pad was built, or cleared, at all 150 LFs and 15 LCFs in the missile complex. At least three fatal helicopter crashes occurred in the Ellsworth missile complex: October 9, 1971; September 1, 1982, and May 29, 1986. (John Mills collection, National Park Service.)

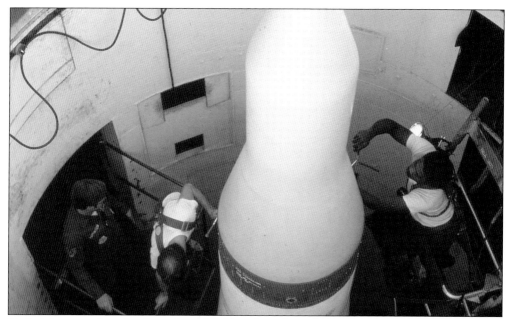

Technicians stand on the diving board (left) and inside a work cage (right) to access the reentry system of a Minuteman II missile. Working inside the launch tube was a careful affair, due to pyrotechnic ordnance installed on the missile, the obvious nuclear warhead, and the drop to the bottom of the silo. (John Mills collection, National Park Service.)

After the removal of the Mark 11 reentry vehicle, the next layer of the missile was the section containing penetration aids, loaded inside three cylinders. Pen aids, as they are known, give the missile a higher probability of success when entering Soviet airspace. During the 1960s, antiballistic missile (ABM) systems near Moscow forced Minuteman designers to find a way to defeat the countermeasures of the "Pushkino Pill Box" (Don-2N) radar. (John Mills collection, National Park Service.)

On December 5, 1964, a maintenance technician used an unapproved tool (a screwdriver) to pull a fuse from sensitive electronic equipment inside Lima-02. According to the accident report, the short circuit caused retrorockets on the rear of the warhead to fire, resulting in the Mark 11 reentry vehicle falling to the bottom of the silo, as depicted in this diagram. The full story of the "Broken Arrow" incident was not revealed for nearly 53 years (US Air Force Safety Center.)

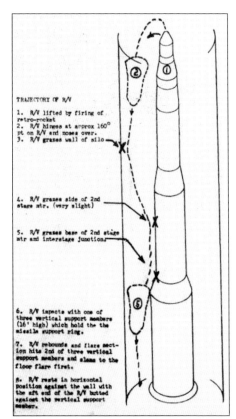

TRAJECTORY OF R/V

1. R/V lifted by firing of retro-rocket
2. R/V hinges at approx 160° pt on R/V and noses over.
3. R/V grazes wall of silo.

4. R/V grazes side of 2nd stage mtr. (very slight)

5. R/V grazes base of 2nd stage mtr and interstage junction.

6. R/V impacts with one of three vertical support members (16' high) which hold the the missile support ring.

7. R/V rebounds and flare section hits 2nd of three vertical support members and slams to the floor flare first.

8. R/V rests in horizontal position against the wall with the aft end of the R/V butted against the vertical support member.

Sgt. Bill West, Security Alert Team leader, stands in front of his vehicle holding his M-16 rifle. Security duty in the missile field required long hours of boredom and driving to distant sites. Usually, the only intruders were rabbits or coyotes, but as anti-nuclear protests became more common in the 1970s and 1980s, human intruders could be found hopping the LF fences. (William West collection, National Park Service.)

A typical crew uniform for 44 SMW personnel shows the missile badge ("pocket rocket") on the left breast pocket, the 44 SMW "Aggressor Beware" patch on the right, and shoulder patches indicating job position (instructor) and higher headquarters' crewmember excellence award. The insignia above the right pocket nametape reads "combat crew." (Bruce Stovall.)

After graduating crew training at Vandenberg AFB, SAC issued certificates such as this to the new missile combat crew members. (Bruce Stovall.)

Strategic Air Command

presents

Missile Combat Crew Member's Certificate

to

2LT THOMAS B. STOVALL JR.

for

Successfully qualifying as DEP MSL COMBAT CREW COMMANDER in the MM-1 ICBM on this 4 day of AUGUST 19 69

AUTHENTICATED BY:

E. B. Wilson

E. B. WILSON
Colonel, USAF
Commander, 44SMW

B. K. HOLLOWAY
General, USAF
Commander in Chief

SAC FORM 136, JUL 66, REV.

A proud crew member beams as he poses in front of the Charlie-01 LCF gate. Opportunities to take photographs on the LCF or down in the LCC were limited, due to the classification of equipment and documents. However, there were few restrictions on hamming it up outside the LCF gate. (National Park Service.)

Crew members inspect the oil level in their vehicle during their post-alert actions after returning to Ellsworth. While a seemingly minor activity, low oil levels could cause damage to the vehicle engine, especially during South Dakota's extremely cold winters. (National Park Service.)

Members of the 44 SMW arrive at Vandenberg AFB to participate in the 14th annual Olympic Arena missile combat competition. The competition pits personnel in operations, maintenance, support, and security forces against the other Minuteman ICBM units around the United States. (Author's collection.)

This faux monetary scrip was created by the 44 SMW for the 1972 Olympic Arena team. During the event, teams would attempt to playfully "steal" pins, patches and other small items from other competitors. (Author's collection.)

This footlocker belonged to a maintenance crew representing the 44 SMW at the 1985 Olympic Arena missile combat competition. Each team created unique storage for their equipment to foster camaraderie within the team and invoke jealously in competitors. (Black Hills Bandits Facebook group.)

The 44th Missile Wing Black Hills Bandits celebrate their victory as the best overall ICBM wing at the 1992 Olympic Arena missile combat competition. This was the final hurrah for the Bandits, as they were in the midst of deactivating their Minuteman II missile systems after President Bush's September 1991 stand-down order. (Author's collection.)

Vice. Pres. George H.W. Bush visited Ellsworth in 1988, touring the missile procedure trainer with First Lieutenants Manny Quinones (left) and Michael Clemente. A few years later, as president, Bush directed a dramatic shift in nuclear weapons policy that would have a great effect on Ellsworth AFB's bomber and missile crews. (National Archives.)

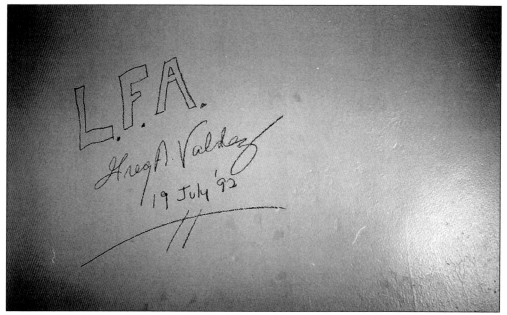

On July 19, 1992, missileer Greg A. Valdez worked his last alert at Delta 01. Inscriptions such as this are a missileer tradition, allowing personnel to celebrate the last time they will (likely) work in an underground LCC. Returning commanders or second-tour personnel may have two or more "LFAs." (Library of Congress.)

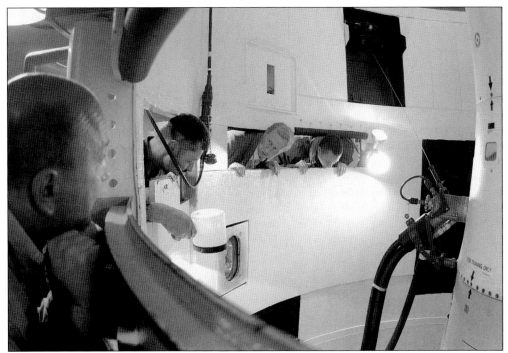

Above, members of the US and Russian START inspection teams look into the launch tube at the 44 MW training LF. The wall cutouts allow missile instructors to point out features and characteristics of the missile's ground equipment. Such wide cutouts do not exist inside operational LFs. Below, Maj. William White, Defense Threat Reduction Agency escort team chief (center), listens to questions from a Russian inspection team linguist. (Both, National Archives.)

SAC constructed training LFs at every Minuteman base to allow maintenance personnel a location to hone their craft. The training LF was a popular spot for distinguished visitors—unlike live LFs containing ladders, the training LF had a large staircase to walk down into the launcher equipment room. (Kent Pillatsch.)

A Minuteman TE sits at the 44 MW training launch facility on Ellsworth AFB. TEs are considered START inspectable items, since many other nations use their missile transporters as launchers also. In the Minuteman system this is not possible, but the TEs are limited in number by treaty anyway. (Kent Pillatsch.)

A National Park Service ranger gives a tour of the Delta-01 LCC. The LCC was kept as it was after the inactivation of the 44 MW. Magazines in the waiting room upstairs and down in the LCC date from the early 1990s, and vintage computer equipment remains in place to show the state of technology at the time. Interestingly, many of the retired components in the LCC are still in use at active LCC facilities in Wyoming, Montana, and North Dakota. (National Park Service.)

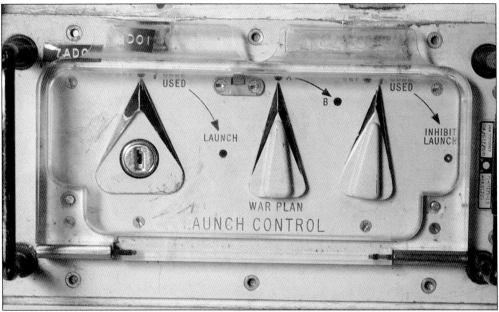

The launch control panel installed at Delta-01 contains three switches. Contrary to popular belief, there is no button. The missile combat crew commander's launch key is inserted at the far left and, with the deputy's key turn, processed as one launch vote. An additional launch vote—provided by another squadron LCC—begins the launch sequence. In case of unauthorized key turns, the inhibit switch (far right) is used to prevent launch. (National Park Service.)

A family reads the placard outside the LF gate at Delta-09. While tourists can visit Delta-09 and take an audio tour, context for the entire Minuteman system is missing without a corresponding visit to Delta-01 and the visitors' center. (National Park Service.).

This view of the Delta-09 LF from inside the launch tube shows the glass cover at the top. START required this modification to show the missile silo is unable to launch an ICBM. Russian satellites provide treaty monitoring, inspecting this LF as well as other START-decommissioned systems to prevent reuse. (National Park Service.)

Leaders from Air Force Global Strike Command and the 20th Air Force perform a ribbon-cutting ceremony with National Park Service personnel to celebrate the grand opening of the new Minuteman Missile National Historic Site visitors' center near Philip, South Dakota, on September 24, 2016. Before these facilities were built, temporary structures were located at Delta 01. (US Air Force.)

The visitors' center at the Minuteman Missile National Historic Site sits on a few acres of land immediately north of I-90, off exit 131. The center helps recognize the mission and purpose of the Minuteman II missile silos that were strategically placed throughout the Great Plains during the Cold War. (National Park Service.)

The logo of the 28th Bomb Wing has remained constant throughout the decades after its creation for the 28th Composite Group on November 14, 1941. The shield contains the colors blue, representing the sky and the primary area where the Air Force operates, and yellow, symbolizing the Air Force's core value of "excellence in all we do." The wavy partition line where the two colors meet makes a cloud-like effect. (Air Force Historical Research Agency.)

Five

ELLSWORTH IN THE MODERN AGE

1992–PRESENT

While the 1990s saw an uptick in aerial action around the world, one Ellsworth mission met its end while another mission shifted drastically. The end of the Cold War began with the 1989 fall of the Berlin Wall and culminated in the December 1991 dissolution of the Soviet Union. The Cold War between the superpowers ended with no (nuclear) shots fired in anger.

In September 1991, Pres. George H.W. Bush directed the safing of all Minuteman II ICBMs. The Air Force also removed Ellsworth's aircraft-delivered nuclear ordnance in 1991, and the 44 MW Minuteman II force was dismantled over the span of three years, ending with the implosion of the last launch facility, Kilo-06, on September 13, 1996.

Sidelined during Operation Desert Storm, Ellsworth's B-1Bs saw their first combat action during December 1998's Operation Desert Fox over Iraq. The four-day military campaign saw 37th Bomb Squadron aircrews strike Iraq's elite Republican Guard, finally proving the lethality of the B-1B in combat.

The Global War on Terror began with the terrorist attacks against the United States on September 11, 2001, and consumed the military might of the United States over the next decade. The 28th Bomb Wing crews saw combat during Operation Enduring Freedom (OEF) in the skies over Afghanistan. During the first six months of OEF, B-1Bs from Ellsworth and Dyess AFB, Texas, dropped 40 percent of the total ordnance delivered by coalition aircraft, including approximately 3,900 Joint Direct Attack Munitions (JDAMs). The B-1B found its niche as a high-precision "bomb truck," providing support in many previously unimaginable roles, such as interdiction and close air support.

Combat technology in the 21st century has seen remotely piloted aircraft (RPAs) routinely flying combat missions. In 2011, the 89th Attack Squadron (formerly the 89th Reconnaissance Squadron of 1942 Doolittle Raid fame) reactivated and began employing MQ-9 Reapers from ground control stations at Ellsworth. This support of worldwide combatant commanders shows how Ellsworth continues to lead the way with a proud heritage and awesome combat capabilities.

In 1988, SAC designated Ellsworth as home of the Strategic Warfare Center (SWC), supervising air tactics training for B-52H and B-1B crews over the Strategic Training Route Complex. (National Archives.)

A B-1B at Thumrait Air Base, Oman, is loaded with munitions before a flight in support of Operation Desert Fox during December 1998. Desert Fox was the B-1's operational combat debut. (Lt. Col. John Martin.)

The aircrew of B-1B (serial No. 86-0102) *Moon Doggie* stand in front of their aircraft at Thumrait Air Base, Oman, on December 19, 1998. From left to right are Capts. John Martin, Joe Reidy, Jeffrey Taliaferro, and Randy Kaufman. The aircraft is marked with a single black bomb (under cockpit window) after the crew's mission to drop ordnance the preceding night. (Lt. Col. John Martin.)

Bomb damage assessment shows the devastation brought by the B-1B's combat debut during Operation Desert Fox in December 1998. The dark circles are impact points for Mark 82 general-purpose bombs. Later conflicts would showcase the B-1B's capability as a bomb truck with precision-guided munitions. (US Air Force.)

AL KUT BARRACKS WEST-NORTHWEST, IRAQ

Mark 82 gravity bombs sit on support beams at RAF Fairford, waiting to be loaded onto a B-1B. Ellsworth B-1Bs deployed to the United Kingdom in support of NATO Operation Allied Force in March–June 1999. (National Archives.)

B-1Bs from the 28 BW sit on the flight line at RAF Fairford in support of Operation Allied Force. The B-1B joined B-52s and KC-135 aerial tankers in a bombing campaign against the Federal Republic of Yugoslavia's armed forces. The airspace was extremely hostile, with B-1 crews counting at least 20 surface-to-air missiles fired at them during their first 50 missions. (National Archives.)

Munitions personnel load a B-1B with bombs prior to a strike on Afghanistan during Operation Enduring Freedom in October 2001. Ellsworth crews deployed to undisclosed locations around the Middle East after the September 11, 2001, attacks on the United States. Commanders and ground troops prized the B-1B's capabilities of long loiter time, heavy payload, and precision strike to assist in close air support operations against insurgents. (National Archives.)

An Air Force member at Diego Garcia (British Indian Ocean Territory) from the 28th Air Expeditionary Wing writes, "What Goes Around Comes Around," on a bomb readied for B-1B and B-52 crews flying during Operation Enduring Freedom. (National Archives.)

Incomplete landscaping is behind newly constructed houses on Ellsworth AFB in 2003. Living in base housing provides young enlistees and officers a chance to experience something beyond a rental but short of full home ownership. In the mid-1990s, Congress pushed for military housing privatization to lessen government costs. (National Archives.)

New homes inside Prairie View await tenants around 2003. Five hundred units of Ellsworth's housing built in the late 1980s/early 1990s were condemned due to settling foundations and cracked walls. The government brought an $8 million fraud case against Hunt Building Corporation, claiming structural and design defects within the Centennial Estates 828-unit housing project. Allegations included violation of fire-safety requirements, construction flaws that caused the houses to twist and break apart in the fierce winds of the high plains, and pipes simply inserted into the ground to make it appear as if they were mandatory sewer clean-outs. (National Archives.)

Air Force members from the 28 BW board a World Airways MD-11 passenger aircraft for transport to a forward deployed location on December 2, 2003. Ellsworth deployed personnel and aircraft to the US central command area of responsibility in support of Operations Enduring Freedom, Iraqi Freedom, and the Global War on Terrorism. (National Archives.)

Ellsworth ground crew members use a Halvorsen 25,000-pound loader to move baggage and equipment onto a World Airways MD-11 aircraft on December 2, 2003. The Halvorsen loader is a high-reach mechanized loader that can lift up to 25,000 pounds of cargo. The loader's name comes from Col. Gail Halvorsen, a cargo pilot during the 1948 Berlin Airlift best known as the "Candy Bomber," dropping chocolate treats to besieged German children. (National Archives.)

Lee Greenwood (left) autographs CDs for Maj. Randy Bass at the Rushmore Plaza Civic Center on March 21, 2002. Major Bass, a 28th Operations Support Squadron weather flight commander, and his family were invited to meet Greenwood prior to the show. (National Archives.)

Becky Hammon (left), a Women's National Basketball Association (WNBA) player, and her brother-in-law Matt Batie give a thumbs-up before a B-1B flight simulator ride on February 13, 2002. Hammon is a native of Rapid City and played for the WNBA from 1999 to 2014. In 2008, she obtained Russian citizenship, playing basketball on the Russian national team in the 2008 Olympics, winning a bronze medal. (National Archives.)

Ellsworth personnel greet First Lady Laura Bush during a visit to South Dakota on November 3, 2002. Bush was in South Dakota to give stump speeches for fellow Republicans prior to local elections. (28th Bomb Wing History Office.)

Master Sgt. Erin Lefever, 28th Aircraft Maintenance Squadron Bomber Task Force (BTF) project officer, stands in front of a B-1B at Andersen AFB, Guam, on January 4, 2021. Ellsworth crews and ground personnel regularly provide support to the BTF during rotational assignments to Guam. (US Air Force.)

Ellsworth family members greet military members returning from a rotational deployment. Temporary duty assignments around the world have become the norm for aircrews, maintainers, and support personnel in the 21st-century Air Force. Arrival at home station is made all the sweeter when family members are there to greet returning deployers. (US Air Force.)

In 2016, Ellsworth's iconic Pride Hangar was renovated to expand the fitness facilities inside and install a turf field for sports. Originally designed to house the monstrous B-36 Peacemaker, the Pride Hangar has provided shelter and support (by various means) to Ellsworth personnel and their families for over seven decades. (28th Bomb Wing Public Affairs Office.)

A retired B-1B (serial No. 83-0067) welcomes visitors to the South Dakota Air and Space Museum (SDASM). The SDASM resides off-base near Ellsworth's main gate to allow the public a peek into the aircraft and weapons used by base personnel throughout the years. Additionally, the museum houses artifacts and exhibits about prominent South Dakotan aviators. (Wikimedia Commons.)

Personnel from the 28th Civil Engineer Squadron install a Titan 1 ICBM outside the SDASM on August 16, 2017. The team took nearly three hours to lift the nearly 12,000-pound missile into a cradle specially designed by a student from the South Dakota School of Mines and Technology. (28th Bomb Wing Public Affairs Office, No. 170816-F-KN558-0118.)

In scenes familiar to any current or former maintenance personnel at Ellsworth, these B-1B aircraft sit among piles of infamous South Dakota snow and ice, waiting for their next flight. (Both, US Air Force.)

On June 21, 2010, Air Force officials announced their decision to locate ground control stations for the MQ-9 Reaper unmanned aerial vehicle at Ellsworth. The MQ-9 provides combatant commanders with actionable precision reconnaissance capabilities for time critical targets, air interdiction, close air support, and strike coordination. This control setup includes the pilot's seat (left) and the sensor operator, with numerous screens displaying video and telemetry from their Reaper. (US Air Force.)

The 89th Attack Squadron (formerly the 432nd Attack Squadron), was activated at Ellsworth on October 1, 2011. The 89th Attack Squadron "Friday" (morale) patch shows a gunman with two pistols behind two aces and two eights, the "dead man's hand" reportedly held by Wild Bill Hickock before he was murdered at Deadwood, South Dakota, in 1876. The Marauders nickname revives recognition of the historic Black Hills notoriety, harkening back to Ellsworth's Cold War–era "Black Hills Bandits." (Author's collection.)

An F-16 Fighting Falcon (above) from the US Air Force Air Demonstration Squadron, also known as the Thunderbirds, taxies toward the runway prior to an air show on October 8, 2003. Below, Thunderbird maintenance personnel wait for their final inspection from visiting Air Combat Command commander, Gen. Hal Hornburg (far right), before beginning their air demonstration. (Both, National Archives.)

Motorcycles line up before riding in the Dakota Thunder Run at Ellsworth AFB on August 6, 2019. Over 170 motorcycle riders rode from the base to Sturgis to participate in the 19th annual Veterans Recognition Ceremony. (28th Bomb Wing Public Affairs Office, No. 190806-F-JM042-088.)

Members of Ellsworth AFB and the Black Hills community gather during a disaster preparedness exercise at Mount Rushmore National Monument on September 20, 2003. The exercise tested local emergency units' responses to acts of terrorism. (National Archives.)

A B-25 Mitchell takes off from the Ellsworth flight line on April 18, 2019. The date marked the 77th anniversary of the Doolittle Raid, a World War II operation to bomb mainland Japan—marking the first offensive action against the Japanese homeland since the attack on Pearl Harbor on December 7, 1941. (28th Bomb Wing Public Affairs Office, No. 161116-F-UP124-027.)

Becky Thatcher (left) and TSgt. William Hatten from the 28th Maintenance Squadron unveil the B-1B *Ruptured Duck* nose art during a ceremony at Wright-Patterson AFB, Ohio, on April 17, 2017. Thatcher is the daughter of the late staff sergeant David Thatcher of the Doolittle Raiders. Pilot Ted Lawson scraped the tail of his B-25 when he pointed the nose of his aircraft too high before takeoff. His aircraft was chalked with the nickname "Ruptured Duck," and later featured a caricature of an angry duck on crutches.

This close-up of the *Ruptured Duck* nose art shows a character familiar to most Americans holding two bombs with emblems from the 34th (left) and 37th Bomb Squadrons. During World War II, Walt Disney Studios–designed insignias appeared on trucks, jackets, and aircraft. The original "Ruptured Duck" artwork featured a cross-eyed duck wearing a leather helmet, staring out over crossed crutches. The current version uses a very angry Donald Duck–like pilot holding two bombs.

SSgt. Anika Dexter, 28th Logistics Readiness Squadron, poses in front of a B-1B at the SDASM on November 10, 2016. Dexter wears traditional Navajo turquoise jewelry, honoring her Diné heritage. With grandfathers serving in World War II and Vietnam, Dexter is the latest member in her family's line of warriors. (28th Bomb Wing Public Affairs Office, No. 161110-F-UP124-011.)

John Moyes, 28th Bomb Wing historian, poses at his desk inside the 28th Bomb Wing headquarters on August 21, 2018. Moyes was a munitions systems specialist before becoming a historian. (28th Bomb Wing Public Affairs Office.)

A 28th Munitions Squadron weapons crew member loads a JDAM onto a transport trailer during a "bomb build" event at Ellsworth on August 28, 2018. Over the course of two days, airmen from the squadron built 12 live munitions and 3 inert training bombs. (28th Bomb Wing Public Affairs Office, No. 180828-F-KN558-0463.)

A 28th Munitions Squadron team won the Air Force Combat Operations competition for Air Force Global Strike Command on February 19, 2019. The team competed at the Air Force level in May 2019 against maintainers from other major commands. The local- and service-level competitions determine who are the best munitions specialists. (28th Bomb Wing Public Affairs Office, No. 190205-F-WN564-0322.)

SSgts. Edward Breen (left) and Michael Pincher write down coordinates during joint training exercise Combat Raider on November 16, 2016. The pair are joint terminal attack controllers (JTACs) from the 5th Air Support Operations Squadron at Joint Base Lewis-McChord, Washington. Exercise Combat Raider took place at the Powder River Training Complex near Belle Fourche, South Dakota. The engagement provided realistic training scenarios for JTACs against a myriad of modern threats. (28th Bomb Wing Public Affairs Office, No. 161116-F-UP124-027.)

A JTAC records a B-1B flyover with a smartphone during exercise Combat Raider. Undertaking a combat role undreamed of during its Cold War–era development, the B-1B has proven an excellent aircraft for supporting ground troops. With an internal load of 24 JDAMs, the B-1B can provide a show of force against adversaries with impressive GPS-guided precision strike capability. (28th Bomb Wing Public Affairs Office, No. 161116-F-IP058-116.)

Col. John Edwards, 28th Bomb Wing commander, greets Secretary of the Air Force Heather Wilson, as she arrives at Ellsworth on June 25, 2018. During her visit, Secretary Wilson toured the new 28th Security Forces Squadron's "Little Defender's Den" and the 28th Maintenance Squadron's state-of-the-art cold spray station. (28th Bomb Wing Public Affairs Office, No. 180625-F-RU464-0001.)

Firefighters from Ellsworth's fire department drive through base housing to promote Fire Prevention Week on October 8, 2016. Team members parade in their vehicles while throwing candy to passersby. Fire Prevention Week illustrates the importance of basic activities, such as changing batteries in smoke detectors and planning a home escape route. Fire Prevention Week is the week of October 9, memorializing the Great Chicago Fire of 1871. (28th Bomb Wing Public Affairs Office, No. 161008-F-SE307-025.)

SSgt. Amanda Williams, a 28th Force Support Squadron food services specialist, begins plating her meal during the Chef of the Quarter cook-off held at the base's Raider Café on December 18, 2018. Each team created three plates for the judges and one for the presentation table. Events such as these increase esprit de corps within the food service ranks and allow the judging audience to experience the chef's best recipes. (28th Bomb Wing Public Affairs Office, No. 181218-F-BH261-0112.)

Airmen from Charleston AFB's 437th Airlift Wing disembark from their C-17 Globemaster III after arriving at Ellsworth on August 1, 2020. Under an agreement called Safe Haven, 11 C-17s from Charleston evacuated South Carolina due to Hurricane Isaias. This was the second evacuation in two years for the Charleston/Ellsworth partnership. In September 2019, C-17s evacuated due to Hurricane Dorian's coastal strike. (28th Bomb Wing Public Affairs Office, No. 200801-F-YM413-0086.)

Military working dog Boris sits on a picnic table at Heritage Lake prior to his retirement ceremony on May 29, 2020. Boris arrived at Ellsworth in 2013 and supported 28th Security Forces Squadron operations at the base and during deployments to Saudi Arabia and Qatar. Military working dogs receive the same respect as their two-legged colleagues at the end of their careers, with a medal and a retirement ceremony. (28th Bomb Wing Public Affairs Office, No. 200529-F-YM413-012.)

Members of the 28th Bomb Wing receive temperature checks prior to a deployment in July 2020. The appearance of the coronavirus disease COVID-19 in the United States in February 2020 prompted changes in daily routines for many Americans, including the military. Social distancing, frequent temperature checks, and face masks helped limit the spread of the virus and have become part of life. (28th Bomb Wing Public Affairs Office, No. 200713-F-YM413-133.)

This is an artist's conception of the forthcoming B-21 Raider in an Ellsworth hangar. On March 28, 2019, the Air Force announced Ellsworth would be home to the first two B-21 squadrons. While looking conceptually similar to the B-2 Spirit flying wing, the B-21 incorporates new technologies to maintain stealth and precision bombing. (US Air Force.)

A B-1B taxis in front of the Pride Hangar, which now states, "Welcome to Raider Country," honoring both Doolittle's Raiders and the newest bomber in the Air Force inventory, the B-21 Raider. (US Air Force.)

BIBLIOGRAPHY

Department of Defense. "Minuteman Missile Sites: Management Alternatives and Environmental Assessment." Washington, DC: Legacy Resource Management Program, 1995. npshistory.com/publications/mimi/srs.pdf.

Larson, George. *Thunder Over Dakota: the Complete History of Ellsworth Air Force Base, South Dakota.* Atglen, PA: Schiffer Publishing Ltd., 2013.

Lewis, Karen. "A Baseline Inventory of Cold War Material Culture at Ellsworth Air Force Base." Volume II-7. Langley AFB, VA: Headquarters, Air Combat Command, 1997.

Mueller, Robert. *Air Force Bases, Volume I: Active Air Force Bases within the United States of America on 17 September 1982.* Washington, DC: Office of Air Force History, 1989. media.defense.gov/2010/Sep/21/2001330255/-1/-1/0/AFD-100921-026.pdf.

National Park Service. "Historic American Buildings Survey: Rushmore Air Force Station." HABS No. SD-21-E. Omaha, NE: Great Plains Support Office. lcweb2.loc.gov/master/pnp/habshaer/sd/sd0000/sd0038/data/sd0038data.pdf.

————. *The Missile Plains: Frontline of America's Cold War.* Omaha, NE: National Park Service Midwest Regional Office, 2003. www.nps.gov/mimi/getinvolved/upload/MIMI%20HRS%202006.pdf.

Ogletree, Greg. "The 4th Airborne Command & Control Squadron." *The ACCA Flyer,* vol. 6, issue 3. Twentynine Palms, CA: SAC Airborne Command Control Association, 2000. sac-acca.org/newsletter/flyer1100.pdf.

Ravenstein, Charles A. *Air Force Combat Wings Lineage and Honors Histories 1947–1977.* Maxwell AFB, AL: Office of Air Force History, 1984. media.defense.gov/2010/Sep/21/2001330257/-1/-1/0/AFD-100921-047.pdf.

Science Applications International Corporation. "Environmental Assessment: Demolition of Munitions Storage Area Facilities at Ellsworth AFB, South Dakota." Ellsworth AFB, SD: 28th Bomb Wing, 2009. apps.dtic.mil/dtic/tr/fulltext/u2/a611139.pdf.

Shaw, Frederick J., ed. *Locating Air Force Base Sites: History's Legacy.* Washington, DC: Air Force History and Museums Program, 2004. www.amc.af.mil/Portals/12/documents/AFD-131018-055.pdf.

United States Air Force. *28th Bomb Wing and Ellsworth AFB History.* Ellsworth AFB, SD: 28th Bomb Wing History Office, 2011. www.ellsworth.af.mil/Portals/146/AFD-110729-042.pdf.

INDEX

ABOUT THE SDASM

The South Dakota Air and Space Museum (SDASM), near the main gate of Ellsworth AFB, contains a number of exhibits displaying South Dakota's aviation history. Indoor galleries contain aerospace exhibits highlighting engineering, innovation, science, and history. Outdoor exhibits display over 30 aircraft types, including models flown by Ellsworth aircrews as well as the South Dakota Army and Air National Guard. Early fighter aircraft—including most of the "Century Series" of fighters—sit alongside their cargo and utility aircraft companions. Three of the museum's prize jewels—a B-1B Lancer, a B-29 Superfortress, and a B-52 Stratofortress—represent decades of American airpower projected from the airbase in the Black Hills.

The SDASM also provides a look into South Dakota's missile heritage, beginning with the HGM-25 Titan I ICBM sites around Rapid City and concluding with the deactivation of the LGM-30 Minuteman ICBM sites in western South Dakota. The museum's EC-135A represents the legacy of the 4th Airborne Command and Control Squadron, as part of the Post-Attack Command and Control System, Airborne Launch Control System, and Looking Glass missions. A full-size Titan I sits in the airpark alongside a Minuteman II, Nike Ajax surface-to-air missile, and an AGM-28 Hound Dog cruise missile. Additional displays include a Minuteman missile procedures trainer, interactive aircraft cockpits for the F-16 and F-106, cockpit and offensive/defensive system operators simulator for the B-1B, and an exhibit describing the Stratobowl balloon launches from South Dakota in the 1930s.

The museum is approximately seven miles east of Rapid City on Interstate 90, just outside the main gate to Ellsworth Air Force Base. Travelers on I-90 eastbound should use exit 67B, while westbound travelers should use exit 67 and follow the signs to the museum.

2890 Davis Drive, Building No. 5208
Ellsworth AFB, SD 57706

N44.133414, W103.073018

605-385-5189 or 605-385-5188

sdairandspacemuseum.com
facebook.com/sdairandspace/

DISCOVER THOUSANDS OF LOCAL HISTORY BOOKS FEATURING MILLIONS OF VINTAGE IMAGES

Arcadia Publishing, the leading local history publisher in the United States, is committed to making history accessible and meaningful through publishing books that celebrate and preserve the heritage of America's people and places.

Find more books like this at
www.arcadiapublishing.com

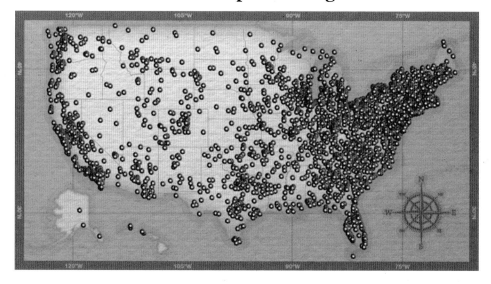

Search for your hometown history, your old stomping grounds, and even your favorite sports team.